DISNEAU

rospective

Robert DOISNEAU

retrospective

Peter HAMILTON

CARTAGO

Published by CARTAGO, London.
An imprint of KEA Publishing Services Ltd.;
63 Edith Grove, London SW10 0LB

Text © 1992 Peter Hamilton
Photographs © Robert Doisneau/Rapho

Designed by Barbara Mercer
Production Coordinator Francesco Venturi

The Cataloguing in Publication data for this book is available from the British Library

Typesetting by August Filmsetting, St Helens
Printed by Amilcare Pizzi, Milan, Italy

ISBN 1-900826-24-0

info@cartago.net www.cartago.net

Exhibition sponsored by J A N N E A U A R M A G N A C

Association Française d'Action Artistique
Ministère des Affaires Etrangères. France.

The Cultural Department of the French
Embassy in London.

The exhibition is being presented in association with 'Visiting Arts'.

Catalogue research supported by Kodak Limited, Professional Imaging.

Recipient of an Arts Council Incentive Funding Award

Registered charity No. 313035: The Museum of Modern Art Oxford receives financial assistance from the Arts Council of Great Britain, Oxford City Council, Oxfordshire County Council, Visiting Arts and Southern Arts.

Contents

Captions: where Robert Doisneau has provided a title in French, this is given first, with an English translation wherever necessary.

captions for pages 1—5

1

Robert Doisneau photographing in the *banlieue*, Montrouge, 1949.

2

Robert Doisneau, London, 1990 (photograph Peter Hamilton).

3

Les Mains de Braque (*The Hands of Braque*), reportage for *Le Point*, Varengeville, 1953.

4

Le Dernier Valse du 14 juillet (*Last Waltz on 14 July*), Paris, 1949.

ACKNOWLEDGEMENTS

I would like to thank the following people for their help and support in the preparation and writing of this catalogue.

Kodak Ltd, Professional Imaging, and especially Paul Gates, for their generous help towards the research and writing. Kathleen Grosset and Raymond Grosset, of the Rapho agency in Paris, without whose support this project would not have been possible. I would also like to thank all the people in the agency, too numerous to name here, who have been so generous with their help and advice with my research on Robert Doisneau's photography. David Elliott and his colleagues at the Museum of Modern Art, Oxford, for their enthusiastic commitment to this project. The Faculty of Social Sciences at the Open University, for help in the initial stages. My wife Susan, and my children, for putting up with me during the trials and tribulations of its realization. Last, but not least, Robert Doisneau and his daughters, Annette Doisneau and Francine Deroudille. To Robert, for opening up his archives so generously for my research, for the many priceless hours spent in his company, and for the chance to share in small part his vision of the world. To Annette and Francine, who have worked tirelessly to collect and prepare so much of the material necessary to both exhibition and catalogue.

Peter Hamilton, Oxford, January 1992

Preface

Pour Peter Hamilton

A ma grande surprise le troisième âge vient de tomber sur mes épaules. Entré dans ce moment de la vie où en principe la mémoire globalise les souvenirs je vois surgir avec précision les détails quotidiens de mes débuts dans la profession.

Mes jeunes confrères ne peuvent imaginer en quel mépris étaient tenus ceux qui avouient se livrer à la photographie, la franchise de ce procédé était considérée comme une obscénité.

Il fallait pour être toléré par ce milieu artistique proposer de fausses gravures ou de simili-pastels. L'uniforme lui-même devait faciliter l'admission dans le cénacle. Personnellement je n'ai jamais porté de chapeau à larges bords ni de veste de velours. Négligeant le port de la barbe j'apparaissais comme un jeune barbare sans éducation ni théories.

J'avais avec des yeux tout neufs une vision aigüe sur les gens et leurs décors, cette joie animale de bien voir je voulais la partager avec d'autres complices puisque les raffinés décadents me tenaient à l'écart.

Dans cet environnement banal qui était le mien il m'arrivait d'apercevoir des fragments de temps où l'univers quotidien paraissait liberé de la pesanteur. Montrer ces moments-là pouvait occuper toute une vie.

Aujourd'hui certains tentent de me donner mauvaise conscience en me qualifiant de prédateur. C'est vrai, je l'avoue, je me suis emparé légèrement des trésors que certains de mes contemporains transportaient inconsciemment, ce qui facilitait mon activité.

Depuis tout est devenu différent, la lecture des images n'est plus réservée à un petit groupe d'initiés. Le sens des métaphores visuelles est partagé par un plus grande nombre.

Je me rejouis en pensant à toutes ces graines glanées au hasard des journées et qui peut-être vont fleurir dans le coeur de nouveaux amis.

Robert Doisneau
Montrouge, jeudi 30 janvier 1992

For Peter Hamilton

To my great surprise the third age has just fallen upon my shoulders.

Entering this time of life when the mind puts all one's memories together, the everyday details of my beginnings in this profession come back to me with great detail.

My younger colleagues cannot imagine with what distaste those who declared their interest in photography were viewed; to be frank about such a thing was considered a sort of obscenity.

In order to be tolerated by the art world you had to make false engravings or imitation pastels. Wearing the uniform should have admitted you to the inner circle. Personally, I never wore a wide-brimmed hat or a velvet jacket, and neglecting to sport a beard I looked like a young savage without education or theories.

With my brand-new eyes I had a clear view of people and their surroundings, and I wanted to share this animal joy of being able to see clearly with others of a like mind, since the refined bohemians wanted nothing to do with me.

In those ordinary surroundings which were my own, I happened to glimpse some fragments of time where the everyday world appeared to be freed of its ugliness. To show such moments could take a whole lifetime.

Nowadays some people try to give me a bad conscience by describing me as a 'predator'. It's true, I will admit, that I gently took hold of the treasures that some of my contemporaries were carrying about quite unawares, and it helped my job.

Since then, everything has changed, and the understanding of images is no longer confined to a small group of the initiated. The meaning of visual metaphors is shared by more people.

I comfort myself with the thought of all those seeds gleaned by chance from such days, which perhaps will flower in the hearts of new friends.

Robert Doisneau

8

In a century which is often characterized by its hostility and alienation, it is a fitting tribute to the work of Robert Doisneau that it is known for its gentleness and humanity. Some of his images have acquired the status of popular icons and one of these, *The Kiss at the Place de l'Hôtel de Ville*, now seems to take pride of place in the bedroom of the archetypical teenager; it has also been widely copied. Doisneau has been paid the ultimate compliment: in this way his work has returned to the streets on which it was made – bootlegged – sold on pavement stalls. Here it has reached, and been purchased by, the public out of which it was born, a public which, paradoxically, would rarely penetrate the galleries of a museum or the glossy pages of a book on photography.

But Doisneau's sympathies have always been with such people and, from the early 1930s, a large part of his work has been devoted to making a record of life on the margins – the suburbs and sparse hinterland between Paris and the countryside. The people in his photographs are also often located in a metaphorical suburbs – a society which is in continuous flux: from reality to fantasy; from passion to boredom; from youth to age; from simplicity to pretension; from innocence to knowledge.

When Doisneau made *The Kiss,* on commission from *LIFE* magazine in 1950, it was published as one of a series of embracing couples which accompanied a predictably written feature about Paris as the world capital of romantic love. It was not the lead picture and the art editor does not seem to have been aware of its destiny. The photograph was, like several others in the sequence, a recreation of something Doisneau had seen earlier but, more real than a documentary record, it has achieved an independent life of its own. Like Rodin's sculpture of the same title, it is now recognized as a representation of universal love.

Photography for Doisneau is a popular art which subverts pretension. He has made portraits of virtually all the leading artistic and literary figures of post-war France, but the most successful show an intuition which transcends the public persona: Picasso perched like a monkey on the end of a couch with Françoise Gilot in the foreground; Jacques Tati against a white background with the constituent parts of a bicycle laid out in chaos on the floor around him. Doisneau feels most affinity, however, with those artists who work outside tradition – outsiders, practitioners of Art Brut or the surrealists whose interest in the child-like mirrored his own.

Perhaps the most memorable of these kinds of photograph rest on the surrealist-inspired idea of the *objet trouvé*: the incongruity of the flower-decked aero-car with a bowler-hatted father accompanying the child driving it (1934); an air-raid shelter stacked with classical statues outside the Louvre (1944); a series of 'art lovers' reacting variously to a nude painting in a gallery window on the rue de Seine (1948); or art transporters vicariously manhandling the large Maillol nudes in the Jardin des Tuileries (1964).

Now at the beginning of his eighty-first year, Doisneau is again working to record the life and spirit of the Parisian suburbs in which he grew up. This catalogue and accompanying exhibition are a tribute to his artistic achievement. While the fabric of Paris has been transformed in the course of his long and ever creative career, the vision of Robert Doisneau, photographer and artist, has remained constant.

David Elliott
Director
Museum of Modern Art
Oxford
1992

5
Engraving made by Doisneau at École
Estienne, requiring about a week's work,
1926.

6

Le Petit Balcon, Paris, 1953.

Introduction

C'est toujours à l'imparfait de l'objectif que tu conjugues le verbe photographier.

(JACQUES PRÉVERT)[1]

The work of Robert Doisneau represents one of the most impressive achievements of the photographic perspective known as *humanistic reportage*. His files contain in excess of 325 000 negatives, made over a period of more than sixty years beginning in 1929, which cover almost any imaginable subject. The majority were made within a relatively small area of Paris and its *banlieue* (suburbs), while the rest were mostly produced in other parts of France, for Doisneau has rarely ventured with his camera beyond the confines of his own country. Yet although Doisneau has returned to certain themes a number of times in his photographic career, the viewer of his photographs is rarely struck by any sense of repetition. This is due more to the fact that Doisneau was constantly seeking the new in his exploration of the visual resources of his surroundings, than to his confirmed habit of never over-shooting a subject. There are rarely more than three or four negatives of a subject subsequently made famous by a Doisneau picture, while certain of his contemporaries were what the French call *mitrailleurs* (machine-gunners), devoting several films to a given subject or reportage theme. Such economy of means has its counterpart in the modesty of Doisneau's character, and is also a feature of his whole approach to the act of photography.

Many of Doisneau's most famous photographs were the outcome of a long wait on a street corner, or a lengthy promenade through a series of locations which might prove productive. Doisneau preferred to describe himself as a *pêcheur d'images*, (a 'fisher' of pictures) rather than to use the term commonly used for reportage photographers – *chasseur d'images* (picture-hunter). The difference is significant. In order to make 'my' pictures, Doisneau has said, 'Il fallait que je me mouille' – 'I had to "get wet", to immerse myself in the life of the people whom I was photographing.' Out of such an approach came the most comprehensive and multi-faceted self-portrait of his social class, a self-portrait which also shows the photographer as a person woven into the fabric of his times.

Doisneau's photographs are the result of patience, reflection, complicity, involvement. Yet in their largely urban subject-matter they also

7
Fox-terrier sur le Pont des Arts (Fox Terrier on the Pont des Arts), the painter is Daniel Pipard, Paris, 1953.

13

8
Robert Doisneau at age 8 (photograph Studio
Albert), Paris 14ᶜ, 1920.

encapsulate a key element of modernity – a modernity first expressed by Charles Baudelaire as a world of the contingent, the transitory, the fleeting, whose quintessential expression is the modern city. And no city is more 'modern' than Paris. Doisneau's pictures present the city with all the ambivalence characteristic of modernism, as both a well-oiled machine and a strange, even magical place. This imagined environment is made up of the symbols, images, metaphors, fantasies and stories which get woven into the fabric of place – a fabric that is the stuff of Doisneau's photography. In some ways his pictures could be said to represent the viewpoint of Baudelaire's modernist *flâneur* (strolling onlooker) whose natural milieu is the ebb and flow of the urban crowd. Discussing his approach, Doisneau often cites the old adage that 'Paris est un théâtre où on paie sa place avec du temps perdu' (Paris is a theatre where your tickets are bought by the passing of time).

Doisneau's photography is above all else rooted in a social milieu, that of the *classe populaire* of Paris and its environs. Taken as a whole, it both traces and celebrates the history, culture, politics and preoccupations of that class over the period from the 1930s to the 1990s. The sense of authenticity which underpins his pictures comes directly from Doisneau's conviction that to take photographs of people, it is necessary to involve oneself in their lives – to talk to them, to joke with them, to share their experiences.

The great appeal of his photography may lie in the fact that Robert Doisneau was able to elaborate a visual style and approach which is the photographic equivalent of the Parisian oral narrative tradition. It is surely not accidental that the great friendships of his life have been with those – like Blaise Cendrars, Jacques Prévert, Robert Giraud, Georges Brassens, Maurice Baquet, François Cavanna, Sabine Azema – who have been artists of the written and spoken word, and whose characterizing feature is a fascination with finding the beautiful, the unexpected, the charming, in the ordinary and the banal. Doisneau's concerns and interests are dealt with in pictures which contain an extremely strong narrative structure, where devices such as comedy, parody, pathos and satire operate to make the moral of the tale more interesting to the viewer.

Unlike certain of his photographer contemporaries for whom painting or music are intimately tied up with their interests in the medium (for example, Henri Cartier-Bresson, Willy Ronis), the great cultural influences on Doisneau's photography are to be found in literature and storytelling. References to *lecture* (reading) or to the *lisibilité* (readability) of his images abound in his own discourse about his photography, and Doisneau himself was more interested in discussions about novels, poetry, plays or film than about painting or sculpture. It is tempting to suppose that his training as a lithographer-engraver, and early work as a lettering artist, encouraged him to see images in terms of the printed or painted word and the simple visual structure of the letters from which it is formed. Words — in stories, novels, poetry, plays — have always offered him the escape route into an imaginary world where the ugliness, banality and oppression which afflict ordinary people in their everyday lives can be transformed and take on redemptive qualities. His lifetime's work as a photographer was in part the attempt to work the same sort of miracle in his pictures.

Take, for example, his photograph (Pl. 49) of Mademoiselle Anita at the Boule Rouge (1951). When she slips off her little bolero jacket to uncover her demure shoulders, she is transformed from a rather ordinary shopgirl into a mysterious creature of the night, perhaps (why not?) a star who has stepped into this rather anonymous dance hall in the rue de Lapp and been caught by the lens of the street photographer (who is by the way just visible in the mirror to the right of the picture). So many stories can be woven from this simple picture, so many tales spun from its central image — for is not Mlle Anita also a reincarnation of da Vinci's Mona Lisa, or Lautrec's *buveuse d'absinthe*?

Paris and its suburbs is the arena in which Doisneau's people play out their roles in the narratives of his photographs, and it provides both the backdrop to their performance and — to a certain extent — the scripts which they perform. His vision of Paris is concerned with how it works on a human level, the mechanism beneath the surface, the skeleton beneath the skin. A book he published with a text by Elsa Triolet in 1957 expresses this motivation so clearly — *Pour que Paris soit* (*So that Paris can exist*). It is full of images which show the life of the city and its suburbs as an organic whole, a mass of individual activities which generate the life and energy of this city, what makes it real and distinctive, yet at the same time magical and strange, unlike any other place on earth.

Although much of Doisneau's work can be read at a superficial level as concerned with the humour and charm which such a perspective uncovers, a closer acquaintance with his photographs reveals a fundamentally subversive, even anarchic, character which mocks authority and denigrates establishment values. Doisneau referred to his spirit of 'insubordination' (or *désobéissance*) many times, and it is clearly present throughout his work as a continuous motivation for so many of his most famous pictures, summed up by his comment to the author '... if I hadn't dawdled near the Louvre when I was supposed to be at an advertising job, I wouldn't have got the chance to photograph the men moving the Maillol statue' (Pl. 75).

9
La Route mouillé (*The Wet Road*) (photograph André Vigneau), 1930. (Courtesy Bibliothèque Historique de la Ville de Paris.)

15

10

Marché aux puces (*Flea Market*), St-Ouen,
Doisneau's first reportage for *Excelsior*, 1932.

Doisneau described himself on a number of occasions as a 'subjective'
photographer, a person who wants to help people see things which will
make them laugh or move them. But if we are to understand this 'sub-
jectivity' it needs to be seen in a more objective context, for Doisneau's
choice of themes, approaches and subject-matter also displays a keen
insight into social change within modern France.

The immediacy and accessibility of many of Doisneau's pictures have
led to his work being considered by certain critics as mainly insubstantial
and ephemeral, romantic and frivolous, ignoring deeper and harsher rea-
lities about conflict and division within French society. The argument of
this essay, and of the exhibition to which it forms the catalogue, is that
although this is a popular view it is also highly misleading, for it ignores
both the social and political context in which Doisneau worked, and
fails to give due weight to the role of his photography in expressing the
identity of important sections of the French working class and *petite
bourgeoisie*.

My aim here is to provide not merely an introduction to Doisneau's
work, but to suggest a way of looking at his photography as a whole, a
perspective on how it hangs together as a coherent body of work. The
essay and exhibition are divided into six main sections, each defined by a
particular period in Doisneau's life:

1912—29: Doisneau's background, social milieu, family, education,
training as lithographer-engraver, his first photographs.

1930—9: Doisneau's first professional photography, at Atelier Ullmann
then with André Vigneau, his work at Renault (1934—9), and his personal
work in the *banlieue*.

1940—4: wartime photography and work for the Resistance.

1945—60: the rise of humanistic reportage photography. Under the
impulse of the post-war *folle soif d'images*, Doisneau's work develops into a
comprehensive celebration and exploration of the life and cultural uni-
verse of Paris, and of working-class and *petit-bourgeois* 'Frenchness'.

1960—78: the decline of humanistic reportage, as television competes
with and ultimately replaces the illustrated press. Doisneau's work
becomes more directed by advertising and commercial commissions.

1978—93: return to reportage, and a series of important projects: the
Loire, the urban landscape of the modern *banlieue*, the communes of
Gentilly and St-Denis.

1912—1939

Robert Doisneau was born in the *banlieue* (suburbs) of Paris, in the town of Gentilly, on 14 April 1912. His father Gaston and mother Sylvie (neé Duval) lived at 8 avenue Raspail, a building which stands to this day and, rather curiously, closely resembles that in *La Stricte Intimité* (Pl. 63). Robert's origins were solidly *petit-bourgeois*. The house was also the work-place and store for the Duval family plumbing business. Gaston Doisneau was a clerk in the firm and had married one of the three daughters of the *patron*. Robert's infancy was passed in an atmosphere impregnated by the values of both a lower-middle-class family business and the working-class craftsmanship of the plumbing trade.

The southern *banlieue* at this time was characterized by small factories and trades interspersed with market gardens, unlike the *banlieue Nord*, where most of the large factories of the *région Parisienne* were to be found. A little river called the Bièvre trickled through Gentilly, running along-side avenue Raspail, and into it flowed all the waste products from the small leather tanning works of the town. None the less the river greatly interested the young Doisneau. It was a place of wonder and mystery despite the smell and brownish colour of the water.

His memory of the river is for some reason inextricably linked with the tragic death of his mother in 1919, when Robert was 7. The Bièvre was the route followed by the pilgrims to St-Jacques de Compostelle in the Middle Ages, and Doisneau's memory of his mother is that she was 'very pious, very mystical', someone 'who gave me the sense of the marvel-lous'.[2] Throughout the rest of his childhood Doisneau felt keenly the lack of a feminine personality to whom he was close, and feels that it made him grow up and marry more quickly than he otherwise would have done. After Sylvie died the situation of Robert's father within the Duval family seems to have been somewhat marginal, for he and his young son were allotted a small apartment in the building. The loss of his mother and their precarious status within the Duval household must surely have been very harsh blows to the fragile personality of a young child. Gaston remarried in 1921 and the family moved to another part of Gentilly.

Doisneau's playground as a child was the streets and wasteland (*terrains vagues*) of the *banlieue*, between Gentilly and Paris. At the time the city was still ringed by the massive forts built during the 1840s — *les fortifs* — and was popularly known as the *zone*, a marginal area of transition between city and suburb. It was populated by a shifting population of gypsies, beggars, casual day-labourers, but also migrants from other parts of France seeking work in the new factories and work-shops devel-

11
Renault Vivasport, Parc St-Cloud. Advertising photograph for Renault on which Doisneau was camera operator, 1937.

LE CLUB DE BOULOGNE-BILLANCOURT DES USAGERS DES
AUBERGES DE JEUNESSE DU CENTRE LAIQUE TE RAPPELLE

LES SEULES VÉRITÉS :

Il n'y a pas de héros : les morts sont tout de suite oubliés.
Les veuves de héros se marient avec des hommes vivants,
simplement parce qu'ils sont vivants et qu'être vivant est une
plus grande qualité qu'être héros mort.
Il ne reste plus de héros après la guerre : il ne reste que des
boiteux, des culs-de-jatte, des visages affreux dont les femmes
se détournent ; il ne reste plus que des sots.
Après la guerre, celui qui vit c'est celui qui n'a pas fait
la guerre.
Après la guerre, tout le monde oublie la guerre et ceux
qui ont fait la guerre.
Et c'est justice. Car la guerre est inutile et il ne faut rendre
aucun culte à ceux qui se consacrent à l'inutile.
JEAN GIONO (29 septembre 1938).

12
Leaflet, with text by Jean Giono, given to
Doisneau when he was mobilized in 1939.

oping around Paris – like Renault at Boulogne, or the foundries and
metalworking industries in St Denis. Housing was in short supply for a
rapidly expanding population, and the *zone* contained many shacks and
slums, but also here and there the little *petit-bourgeois pavillons* with
their neatly railed-off gardens. Gradually the *fortifs* began to be dis-
mantled, and new buildings went up, notably the *Habitations à Bon
Marché* (HBM), blocks of workers' flats which began to ring the city
with their concrete and brick towers. The *zone* and its *fortifs* was the
landscape of Doisneau's childhood, a transitory and marginal wasteland
where as he has said 'you went to play, to make love or to commit
suicide'. None the less it fascinated him, and the feeling that it was a
transitory and fleeting place of which he must *inscrire les décors* (record
the surroundings) was with him from an early age.

School in Gentilly's Ecole Communale was not a happy experience for
Doisneau, and a disappointment for his parents, but at the age of 13 he
passed an examination to gain entry to a craft school, the Ecole Estienne in
the 13th *arrondissement* of Paris. The Estienne was the trade school for the
printing industry, and his family thought that at least he would be able to
learn a skilled trade. They would have preferred him to be an engineer,
but a skill, a craft, that was at least a respectable job for a *petit bourgeois bien
élevé*.

From 1925 to 1929 Doisneau learned to become a lithographer-
engraver. He describes the training as preparing him for a job which may
have existed when the teachers were taken on by the school, but which by
1929 was almost totally defunct. 'I could do a wine label showing the
medals won at the Concours agricole of 1900, but nothing useful.' Doisneau was, however, a skilled draughtsman, interested by shapes and
forms, and by the images made by letters, and he had at least been trained
in the relatively useful art of hand-lettering. This enabled him – after a
brief period at a back-street engraver's in the Marais – to find in late 1929
a job as a lettering artist in a Parisian graphic art studio, the Atelier
Ullmann. The Estienne had supplied a limited if very academic type of art
school training, and Doisneau had enjoyed this sufficiently to want to
continue, and attend evening classes in life drawing and still-life in Mont-
parnasse. The years passed in the laborious activity of engraving, working
on a tiny area of stone with a powerful magnifying glass, had given him a
powerful urge to go out on the streets of Paris and the *banlieue*, to capture
the reflections of the water coursing down the gutters, to show the
vibrancy of life in the streets, of people moving through the metropolis.
Even at the Estienne he had been sufficiently disappointed with his drawing abilities to wonder whether photography might allow him to do this.

A borrowed camera, a few promenades through the *terrains vagues* of his childhood, and Doisneau had made some pictures which began to *inscrire les décors* in a more satisfactory manner. These pictures, which date from late 1929 and early 1930, show such subjects as a pile of paving stones, a broken bicycle wheel, the cast-iron gratings around the foot of a Parisian tree, posters on a wall (Pl. 28). There are no people in these pictures, for Doisneau was too shy to approach them. He had wanted to draw them, and had originally thought that the camera would make it easier to do so. He rapidly realized this was not possible.

These pictures also show us that Doisneau's *désobéissance* put in an early appearance. He says that the camera seemed to him then as an 'engin qui permettait la désobéissance' (a 'machine which encouraged insubordination') for it enabled him to enter a visual world which was wholly new and different from the official art so beloved of his masters at the Estienne – for whom Impressionism was just a passing and rather ugly fad. It is interesting that all this was happening during the rise of surrealism in France, but Doisneau was on his own account not aware of the movement. His interests were more firmly focused on literature.

Reading – and Doisneau had always devoured books – offered an escape into a world of magic and fantasy for a lonely and unhappy child. Books also nourished the man, and continued to do so until the end of his life. The stories he enjoyed as a child were frequently escapist, but they included the classics of French literature, like Victor Hugo's *Les Misera-bles*. Doisneau was also attracted to writing which dealt with the subversion of social norms, and fondly remembers Jacques du Val's *Sabre de bois*, a novel about a soldier who is discharged for myopia. Particularly important in his reading was Jean Giono (1895–1970), one of the first writers in France to evoke the horrors of the First World War in *Le Grand Troupeau* (1931). Giono made his name with novels and stories of pastoral life, usually set in Provence, which use a rich and poetic language to evoke in a highly imaginative way the hard life of those who live close to nature, such as *Colline* (1928) and *Jean le Bleu* (1933). Reading satisfied an intellectual streak in Doisneau's personality, for he also dipped into the philosophical literature – even struggling through Montaigne – and later tackled the great works of Marxism.

Doisneau's decisive move into photography as a profession came at the Atelier Ullmann. The studio specialized in advertising artwork for the pharmaceutical industry. Under the impact of modernist trends in graphic design, photography was becoming increasingly used in advertising work, and Ullmann decided to install a darkroom and acquire a camera, lenses and lights. A young man called Lucien Chauffard was given the responsi-

13

Un Physicien dans le vent (Physicist in the Wind/A Fashionable Physicist), part of series made for Maximillien Vox's *Les Nouveaux Destins de l'intelligence*, 1942.

bility for this work, but soon had an unofficial assistant, fascinated by the possibilities of this new medium. When Chauffard left, Doisneau was asked if he would like to take over. His first pictures were judged acceptable (but are in fact of a remarkable standard for a complete beginner). Almost by default Doisneau had become an advertising photographer. At the time the status of the photographer was extremely low – 'someone who might just be asked into the kitchen for a glass of vin ordinaire,' as Doisneau puts it. The family were not pleased, and one of Doisneau's aunts continued to introduce him as 'my nephew the engraver' for many years rather than admit that such a person could be part of her family.

The confirmation of his new role, a turning-point in Doisneau's life, came in 1931 when he went to work as an assistant (*opérateur*) to André Vigneau. 'It was very important for me,' Doisneau has said, 'for Vigneau talked to me of another painting, another philosophy, another cinema. At the time Soviet films were banned, you could only see them in secret, we watched them like conspirators in a locked hall, films like *Battleship Potemkin, Land,* etc.' By a curious coincidence it was Chauffard who had suggested Doisneau for the job – and it was not to be the last favour he would do for his friend. Doisneau was introduced to a world of modernism and avant-garde culture. Vigneau made advertising and fashion photographs but also produced fashion-store dummies, cartoon films, sculpted, painted and played the cello. The studio was very modern in design for Vigneau was in the circle of Le Corbusier and a number of other modernist designers.

> There was a Picasso engraving on the wall, a camera and special table for making cartoons, a statue by Vigneau of a golfer on the loggia of the first floor. On my first day I went into the darkroom to find out where everything was, check out the developing tanks and so forth. There was a door at the end of the darkroom, and I thought I'd better check what's in this cupboard, opened it and who should I find but Vigneau completely nude under the shower! He said, 'Mon Cher, we'll meet shortly.' It was a sign of my destiny.

Vigneau's photography was as modernist as his decor, and his approach was as much influenced by the ideas of the Hungarian and German photographers like Kertesz, Brassaï, and Germaine Krull as by surrealists like Maurice Tabard or Man Ray. Brassaï's book *Paris de nuit* had appeared in 1933, and was a great critical success. Doisneau was so excited by it that he tried to make some similar pictures. But it was one of Vigneau's pictures in particular which made a lasting impression on him: *La Route mouillé* (Pl. 9), for it seemed to express everything about what the 'new'

photography of modernism could be – an impression, a feeling, a subjective reaction of the person viewing the scene, and translated via the mechanical process of photography into something which others could see and feel. Doisneau contrasts it with another sort of 'postcard' photography common at the time, in which the sky was always dark, the clouds were always fluffy 'cauliflowers', the trees were always replete with leaves, the whole beautifully composed but emotionally dead. Vigneau's picture is the reverse of all these conventions: for Doisneau 'it was a sort of photographic *désobéissance*'.

The experience of working with Vigneau created what Doisneau now likes to call a *fumier* (a compost), fertile ground in the young man's mind that another viewpoint was possible which broke with the sterile academicism of the Ecole Estienne and the stifling values of the *petit-bourgeois* world.

> That studio was an enchantment. Vigneau was always saying these things which stunned me, such uncommon things like 'the key board of a typewriter is such a beautiful thing that all love letters should be written on the machine,' or talking to me about the Bauhaus, Surrealism, Le Corbusier's 'machine à habiter,' Soviet cinema....But on technique he was a great bluffer. He would say to me, 'Doisneau, do you think with a gamma[3] of so and so you will get a better result?' I had no idea of what we could do with this bloody gamma – and neither did he!

It was at Vigneau's studio that Doisneau first encountered Jacques and Pierre Prévert (who were then involved in the left-wing theatre group Le Groupe Octobre), and the novelist Georges Simenon,[4] and where he began to master the use of artificial light to 'caress the form' *à la* Vigneau.

By now Doisneau had acquired his own camera, an early Rolleiflex 6×6 cm which allowed direct vision of the scene, rapid action, a fine Zeiss Tessar lens and 12 pictures per roll of film – and was making photographs in the *banlieue* around Gentilly and in Paris in his spare time. He was also courting a local girl from a Protestant family, Pierrette Chaumaison.

The inspirations of Vigneau's photography combined with the continuing desire to *inscrire les décors* drove Doisneau to become a little bolder with people. The famous picture of the two tiny children going to collect the milk (Pl. 35) made in 1932 clearly illustrates Doisneau's frustrations with the ugliness and oppressiveness of the *banlieue* as an environment, the massive scale of the buildings contrasting so starkly with the children's minute proportions. There are many shots from this time of children (Pls.

30 and 36), either playing in the streets and parks of Paris, or in the *terrains vagues* of the *zone*. There are also some pictures of adults, but they tend to be taken from a distance, or from behind (Pl. 29), while the more close-up shots often feature old people. A series of pictures Doisneau made at the *marché aux puces* (flea market) of St-Ouen, which are mostly in this genre, were published by *Excelsior* magazine in 1932, and form his first published reportage (Pl. 10). Another picture, again from 1932 (Pl. 34), shows two women on a market porter's *diable* (handcart) at Les Halles, and demonstrates Doisneau's fascination with the workings of the city, but a certain detachment from the subject which characterizes his early work with all but children.

The period of cultural immersion at André Vigneau's studio in the Quartier Latin came to an end with Doisneau's call-up for military service in 1932. He was stationed in the Vosges and army life only confirmed the nascent anti-authoritarianism in his character. But on his return to Paris, he was not able to return to his job. Vigneau had overstretched himself and in the difficult financial conditions of the early 1930s the studio was going broke.

By good fortune Doisneau ran into his friend Lucien Chauffard (back to camera Pl. 32), now in charge of the photography section at Renault and able to pull a few strings so that he could join the new advertising department at the Boulogne-Billancourt factory as a photographer. The next five years (1934 to 1939) were spent working for Renault, and they were an important phase in his development as a photographer. The move to a salaried post in the company in June 1934 also coincided with the marriage of Robert and Pierrette, on 28 November of that year. The young couple soon moved to a modern apartment in Montrouge, near the Place du Marché. Perhaps still under the spell of the exciting world of Vigneau, they chose a first-floor flat with high north-facing windows, in a block designed as artists' studio-flats at the time when many still lived in the *banlieue Sud*, and it remained Doisneau's home to the end of his life. The painter Fernand Léger lived two doors away.

Gentilly and Montrouge are neighbouring communes, but the great road to Orléans (now the N20) passes close by the Place du Marché. Access to Paris via the Porte d'Orléans was near at hand, while the trip to the factory on the Ile de Seguin could be made by bus. Doisneau thus became part of the great crowd of workers who converged on the factory each day. This and the activity of illustrating the great factory at work gave him a profound respect for those who earn their living through physical labour. He soon joined the CGT (the Confédération Général du Travail), because of all the unions present in the factory 'it was the most left-wing'.

15
Au Bon Coin, St-Denis, 1945.

"MY CAMERA EXPOSURE WAS FIVE SECONDS, THE KISS TOOK SOMEWHAT LONGER," SAYS PHOTOGRAPHER. PASSERS-BY CAUSED BLURS

SPEAKING OF PICTURES . . .

In Paris young lovers kiss wherever they want to and nobody seems to care

Paris is understandably proud of its reputation as the home of fine wines, fine perfumes—and of love. It is a reputation, so far as love is concerned, that is not left to take care of itself: constant practice keeps up the standards. In other cities bashful couples usually seek out parks or deserted streets for their romancing. But in Paris vigorous young couples, determined to uphold the municipal honor, can be observed in unabashed courting in even the most crowded parts of the city.

It goes on all day, this public kissing, and all night too. But Photographer Robert Doisneau, who took the unposed pictures on these pages, found two peaks in the day's osculation: 1) at noon, when offices, shops and universities are closed for lunch and thousands of youngsters are released into the streets, and 2) between 5 and 7 p.m., when young males make the opening moves in the evening's campaign. Only tourists pay any attention to the smooching. The French public ignores it completely, smiles approval even when it gets in the way. One policeman explained, "It is a fine thing, and it keeps these young lads out of trouble. If they weren't with their girls, they would probably be out on some hockey field where they might get hurt."

16

16a&b

First use of the *Baiser de l'Hôtel de Ville*, in *LIFE* magazine, 1950.

intended to show that France, despite its reduced circumstances, was still at the forefront of science.[6] Doisneau made portraits of a number of leading figures such as the Joliot-Curies and the Prince de Broglie, and each one marries a sense of fun with an acute eye for character. His *Un Physicien dans le vent* (Pl. 13) is a representative image from this commission, but it also demonstrates that he had already acquired the formidable visual skills which he was to practise in the post-war period. Vox's book, replete with a number of Doisneau's photographs, was published in 1942, but its sales in this period of penury were not helped by the Preface provided by Marshal Pétain.

For much of the Occupation Doisneau used his photographic and graphic art skills for a somewhat less innocuous purpose: as a forger of documents for the *Resistance*.

> One day in 1941, a guy came to see me and asked me to make a copy of a police inspector's card. I acted as if I didn't understand what he wanted, but in the end I knew that this was a job from the communist *Résistance*, so I did it. From then on I would get all sorts of jobs to do, identity cards, *Ausweis's*, passports, false papers for Jews. We even put up a guy who had been chased by the police all the way from the Porte d'Orléans. One man even left a suitcase full of guns in the apartment! Then one day they came to see me and said, 'we don't need you any more, we've got a more industrial system for forging papers.'

The Resistance work took up much of the night, and must have been a great strain. Pierrette was pregnant with their first child, Annette (born in 1942), and with a young family it was very hard to survive. Doisneau thought he only made about 220 francs from all his forging work, and it almost certainly did not cover the material costs of the papers supplied. But in one sense to be part of the Resistance was also to manifest *désobéissance* and thus it suited Doisneau's character. It also brought him into contact with Communist militants from the world of the arts and literature. Doisneau struck up a close friendship with the painter Enrico Pontremoli, who operated a secret press in the Opéra quarter (see Pl. 40), and together they took part in the liberation of Paris.

Doisneau's files contain almost no photographs of violence or conflict, save for the pictures he took in August 1944 during the Resistance's battle with the German army for control of Paris. This is a fascinating collection of pictures (see magazine spread Pl. 39), some of which were widely published in the American press. Doisneau returned in 1947 to the same locations to contrast the scenes of conflict with those of peace, and although the viewer is immediately struck by the impact of the war pictures, those of 1947 seem to have a more lasting quality to them. He felt that it was too easy to make pictures of hate or violence or even extreme poverty. These are pictures which are immediately *lisible* – readable – and admit of only one interpretation. His preference was for those pictures which are far more difficult to make, in which the combination of creativity, chance, play, even *désobéissance*, contrives to produce a magical effect.

1945–1960

Doisneau sold most of his photographs of the liberation of Paris in 1944 to American newspapers and magazines. The plans he had laid in 1939 to become a reportage photographer could now be put into effect. He joined ADEP, a cooperative agency. Founded in the 1930s by Maria Eisher, Pierre Boucher and René Zuber, when it was known as *Alliance-Photo* the agency briefly attracted many of the leading names of French photography to become members, and there Doisneau met Cartier-Bresson, the *frères* Seeberger, Pierre Jahan, and a number of other photographers who would mould humanistic reportage[7] photography in the post-war era.

The immediate post-war period was characterized by the French public's seemingly unslakeable thirst for illustrated magazines (*Paris-Match, Réalités, Point de Vue, Régards*, etc). This *folle soif d'images*, as it has been called, seems to have been in large part a response to the agonies and deprivations of the war years. Its most apparent feature is the search for a quintessential Frenchness, a means of picturing France and the French which could help to heal the wounds of a society divided by war, defeat, occupation, collaboration and resistance. The visual approach and social perspective of humanistic reportage produced the images which such a market demanded. Humanism, in this context, means the representation of major issues and concerns through their impact on specific individuals who are shown as the agents of their own destinies. It was a reaction against those totalitarian ideologies and impersonal economic forces which tend to treat people as a monolithic and de-individualized mass.

Although this approach is most characteristically and dynamically displayed in the magazines and books of the period 1945–60, its roots are clearly visible in the new wave of reportage photography for the mass-market illustrated magazines which appeared in the 1930s. It was during this period that the role of professional editorial photographer was

19
Jacques Tati, portrait made in *Vogue* studio, Paris, 1949.

created, and in which the modern image of the photo-journalist pacing the streets, Leica in hand, in search of the 'decisive moment', was defined. It was a role which had close connections to modernism's love affair with the city, but it also owed a good deal to surrealism's attempt to destroy the distinction between subjective vision and objective reality. In Brassaï's *Paris de nuit*, for example, the photographer takes on the role of *flâneur*, spy and witness of the hidden life of the modern city. Kertesz's reportage work for *Vu* develops the idea that pure photography should 'hide both a distortion and a subjective stand', enabling the photographer to impose his vision on the world and its minutiae.

The new magazines of the post-war era could not compare in quality with their pre-war counterparts, but in the scope and multiplicity of the subjects which they treated, they were far ahead. They also allowed a freer rein to the expression of political values (and particularly a commitment to the *classe populaire*) on the part of the photographer.

Many of the photographers within the humanistic reportage group shared a left-wing perspective on the social changes underway in post-war France, and some of their photographic projects attest to a more subversive and questioning approach to the 'new France'. At the same time those images of joy, pleasure, happiness, romance which appear so frequently among the work of the group also support the notion that they shared an essentially optimistic and positive perspective on human nature, and a belief in its ability to surmount hardship and handicap. A more considered view would argue that the approach of the photographers is one in which both an optimism about social reconstruction and a pessimism about its effects seem to be balanced. A second or more reflective look at so many of the photographs of Doisneau, or of his contemporaries Willy Ronis or Izis for example, shows them to have a harder, colder, more ambiguous or melancholy edge.

The 'harder' edge of French humanistic photography is due in part to the fact that most of the generation who made up this school became reportage photographers before 1939, and in some cases worked as staffers or freelancers for one or other of the Communist or far-left magazines. Their pre-war subjects included strikes, riots, or social disorder, but they were interspersed with pictures portraying the lifestyles and labour conditions of the French working class – Cartier-Bresson's iconic *The Banks of the Marne*, and Doisneau's Renault workers at their *casse-croûte* (meal-break) typify this approach. The work indicates a clear political identification with the working class, which is carried into the post-war era. But as that class became more secure and affluent its portrayal through the reportage of the humanists also evolved, so that the ironies

20

Les Pains de Picasso (Picasso's Bread), reportage for *Le Point*, Vallauris, 1952.

and ambivalences of its *embourgeoisement* became increasingly their subject-matter. The humanistic photographers also confined themselves largely to France, their work carried out within its boundaries (Henri Cartier-Bresson, Jean-Philippe Charbonnier and Edouard Boubat being the major exceptions to this rule). As a result, the wider problems of France in an era of decolonization– wars in Indo-China and Algeria – are less prominent in their work.

Doisneau's post-war career as a freelance *photographe-illustrateur* is marked by a number of important associations which enabled him to marry his photographic perspective to a series of fruitful projects. Through ADEP he encountered Pierre Betz, the editor and jack-of-all-trades of a subscription journal called *Le Point*. Each edition was devoted in its entirety to a particular theme – the work of a painter, a sculptor, a writer, etc. Over the period from 1945 to 1960 Doisneau worked on a number of editions of the journal, each one superbly printed and beautifully designed: The commissions from Betz enabled Doisneau to meet some of the major cultural figures of the period, and led to some of his finest work, in particular the portraits of Picasso (Pl. 20) and Braque (see title page Pl. 3, and Pl. 41), but also a fine shot of the writer Léautaud; and some wonderful interiors of bistros, for an issue written by his friends Jacques Prévert and Robert Giraud.

In 1945 Doisneau began to work for another review, a broadsheet journal of 'crypto-Communist' inclinations edited by Pierre Courtade called *Action*. At about the same time he was asked to go to Aix-en-Provence by Maximilien Vox, to make a portrait of the novelist Blaise Cendrars (1887–1961), whose *L'Homme foudroyé* was shortly to be published. This meeting was to produce Doisneau's first book, but it had a far more important function in that it confirmed for the first time to Doisneau that his personal project, to *inscrire les décors* of the *banlieue* was itself a worthy enterprise. As I have argued in the introduction, Doisneau's photographs of the people of Paris and the *banlieue*, the *menu peuple* or 'ordinary folk', are a sort of double self-portrait: of a social class and of Doisneau himself. Of *La Banlieue de Paris*, Doisneau has remarked '. . .it is my portrait. Like the book, I am a mixture of rubble and slag'.[8] (See the portrait of Doisneau as 'photographe de banlieue' in the frontispiece, Pl. 1.) Cendrars warmed to the young photographer, perhaps because Doisneau, the avid reader, knew his work. They talked about the *banlieue*. As Doisneau has remarked of this meeting, 'it's far more common to talk with nostalgia of Aix-en-Provence in Kremlin-Bicêtre or Villejuif than the other way around'.

Cendrars and Pierre Courtade were the first people to look at Doisneau's pictures of the *banlieue* and find them interesting, although for different reasons: Courtade saw the pictures as a sort of condemnation of the *petite bourgeoisie's* attachment to the values of property, while Cendrars had a rather bleaker view of the poverty – material, cultural, intellectual – to which he felt they pointed. The book was Cendrars's idea, and he would write to Doisneau regularly during its production, for he thought that the photographer should cover a wider field than his own area. None the less he wanted Doisneau to take all the credit, and in a letter of March 1949 Cendrars writes:

> Mon cher Doisneau,
> I received your photos. Continue to do what you want and don't take any notice of my text. The photos are the main thing, and inspire me to write. This album must be your own book. You are a genius. Understood?

Doisneau did what Cendrars wanted, trailing along the canal d'Aubervilliers (Pl. 15), visiting the gazometers of the plaine St-Denis, and the factories of la Courneuve. In many ways the book was a model for the projects which Doisneau most enjoyed, where he has worked with a writer who possessed a strong point of view, and for whom his photographs could serve as a creative stimulus. Of course the flow of creativity is two-way, as the letters from Cendrars demonstrate, replete with their precise instructions: 'I believe that a photo taken from the train on the line Montparnasse-Versailles, or from the electric Invalides-Versailles wouldn't go badly in the album.' Cendrars also seems to have been responsible for the sections in which the pictures were assembled – *Gosses* (Kids), *Amour* (Love), *Décors* (Surroundings), *Dimanches et Fêtes* (Sundays and Holidays), *Loisirs* (Leisure), *Travail* (Work), *Terminus* (End of the Line), *Habitations* (Housing). He wrote the captions, which often strike a wrong note when Doisneau's versions are seen.

A substantial number of the pictures used in *La Banlieue de Paris* date from the 1930s and include some of Doisneau's earliest photographs – the two children collecting the milk of 1932 (Pl. 35), for example. Certain of the photographs were made at the suggestion of Cendrars, but the great majority derive from Doisneau's personal vision. It is clear that despite their complicity, Cendrars and Doisneau saw things rather differently, the photographer being less harsh in his judgements, concerned more with the possibility of seeing beauty in the banal than the writer, who made it clear in another letter that for him the *banlieue parisienne* was where 'poverty impregnates everything, and still stinks like the first time I set foot there'.

21
Diono le dresseur de chiens (Diono the dog-trainer), Paris, 1946.

33

elle tourne...   elle vole...   elle virevolte..

t rest parfaite à chaque heure de la journée, la robe en Flip ou Double Flip de **LESUR**

22

Magazine advertising photograph using modified Speed-Graphic and turntable, 1964.

The reasons for the differences between them lie perhaps in Doisneau's identification with, and *political* commitment to, the *classe populaire*. From 1945 until 1947 (for much of the time when he was working on *La Banlieue de Paris*) he was a member of the PCF – mainly because close friends had asked him to join. Although it is clear that he was not happy as a *militant de base* – his *désobéissance* always got in the way of any attempt to involve him in disciplined political action – Doisneau felt a close affinity with the working class and *petite bourgeoisie*, whether or not he was a member of a political party or trades union. 'I look like them, I speak their language, I share their conversation, I eat like them. I am competely integrated into that milieu. I have my own work which is a bit different from theirs, but perhaps I am a sort of representative of that class.' From the immediate post-war period Doisneau regularly carried out reportage work for several of the PCF organs such as *Régards* and *L'Humanité*, as well as the CGT magazine, *La Vie Ouvrière*. He retained an admiration for craftsmen and all those who work with their hands – perhaps Cendrars picked this up, for he refers to Doisneau quite often as an 'artisan' in *La Banlieue de Paris* – and many of his finest photographs are concerned with the exercise of a manual craft or simply illustrate hard physical labour (for example, Pls. 72 and 73).

Certain photographs in *La Banlieue de Paris* were *mises en scène* rather than strictly documentary pictures, a technique Doisneau has developed over the years, and which reveals his fascination with the *fantastique social* (finding the fantastic and magical in everyday life). He would frequently observe something happening, but be unable to record it with his camera, later trying to re-stage what he had seen – as in *Le Baiser de l'Hôtel de Ville*. A classic example is the picture which Cendrars captioned as *Dans le train de Juvisy*, and describes as the 'worker who has been to the Quai aux Fleurs and brought back a rose-tree complete with its clod of earth' whom Doisneau will later 'peer over a wall to surprise, at home, in the process of fondly planting his rose-tree'. The 'worker' is M. Barabé, who lived from the 1930s until quite recently on the ground floor of the same building as Doisneau. He appears in many other Doisneau pictures, worked for years as his assistant, and on occasion even looked after his children.

The case of M. Barabé is instructive, for it shows us with what skill Doisneau sought to present his own perspective on the *classe populaire*. This is not to suggest that Doisneau systematically invented 'his' world, but it is to note the creative or subjective dimension which his social photography of the *banlieue* and of the *classe populaire* contains.

In 1946 Doisneau met Raymond Grosset, who had decided to take over the Rapho agency when Rado did not want to return to France after the war. The ADEP agency had proved a total failure as a source of income for Doisneau, and the impeccable honesty and commitment of Grosset to selling the pictures produced by his star photographer persuaded Doisneau to stay with Rapho when Cartier-Bresson asked him to join a new agency, Magnum, in 1947. Rapho suited Doisneau, because it gave him the security and the variety of work which he enjoyed, without having to leave his native country. With a young family (a second daughter, Francine, was born in 1947), and a distaste for grand reportage in the four corners of the world, his work as a freelance *photographe-illustrateur* for Rapho responded to both his temperament and his needs.

The series of important encounters continued with Jacques Prévert, (1900–77) in 1947. Grand surrealist, poet, songwriter, scriptwriter for directors such as Jean Renoir (*La Partie de campagne*, 1936), Marcel Carné (*Quai des Brumes, Le Jour se lève*, 1938–9, *Les Visiteurs du soir*, 1941, *Les Enfants du paradis*, 1945) Prévert may have helped to further unlock the floodgates of Doisneau's imagination, encouraging him to explore the curiosities of a Paris which lay only a bus ride away from Montrouge. The 'great idea' of surrealism was that subjective and objective reality are in fact indistinguishable: Jacques Prévert certainly took that idea as far as it could go, and it increasingly infuses the photography of Doisneau (Pl. 68).

The meeting with Prévert led to a number of unplanned but extensive tours through Paris.

Jacques would ring up and say, 'do you know the street where they unroll the big lengths of plywood near the Faubourg St. Antoine?' I would say 'yes', and he would say 'no you don't, come and get me and we'll go there.' So we would go and look at this, there would be whole logs of this stuff, we'd take in the sound of the work, the colour of the wood, the smell of the sap and the look of it as it came out.

Prévert taught me to have confidence in the discovery of every-day objects which people didn't see any more, because they were contemptuous of them, too used to them. He found ordinary words, used everyday, and presented them to people as if they were precious jewels. And he loved to play, to discover new things, the names of streets for example. 'Why do the worst streets have the prettiest names?' he would say, and I would begin to hear the music of their names – La rue des Cinq Diamants, La rue du Dessous des Berges, La rue du pont aux Biches, Le Passage de la Main d'Or . . .

35

23
Montage, Pont des Arts, Paris, maquette for
large work commissioned by the Mairie de
Pantin, 1971.

Prévert helped Doisneau to find within the streets of Paris pictures which showed the city both as a machine and as a place where magic and fantasy lay just around the corner. They fused their 'imagined environments' of the city into a shared and magical vision, which continued to inspire Doisneau's photography to the end. Doisneau and Prévert were *flâneurs* in precisely the sense Baudelaire intended, and the pictures made during the period of their walks around Paris together are highly revealing of this combination of modernism and surrealism.

Prévert and Doisneau never produced a book together, but did collaborate on an issue of *Le Point* in 1960, dealing with bistros. None the less the fruits of their collaboration, a sort of elective affinity between the artist/writer and the photographer, are evident in the increasingly distinctive photographs which Doisneau made from the late 1940s onwards. By this time he was also part of a wider group loosely associated with Prévert, for he had formed friendships with two interesting figures, Maurice Baquet (Pl. 77) and Robert Giraud.

Baquet – actor, comedian, cellist, skier – had been a member of the Groupe Octobre in the 1930s, and had appeared in a number of the Préverts' films and entertainments. Doisneau and Baquet had been friends since the 1940s, collaborating on a book which finally appeared in 1981 – *Ballade pour violoncelle et chambre noire* – in which Doisneau's *mise en scène* portrait style was taken to its extremes (Pls. 54 and 87). During the 1940s and early 1950s Doisneau's portraiture became increasingly liberated from conventional approaches and sought the elements of chance and fantasy which the 'game' produces. Wherever possible, Doisneau invites his subject to play out a fantasy, pushing at the limits of social convention to invite chance to play as big a part as possible in the picture. The received influence of surrealism probably played a large part in this, but it is also a reaction to the disciplines imposed on the photographer by certain of his commissioned work for advertising or editorial use.

Doisneau's encounter with the writer Robert Giraud was to produce an important body of work, precisely because it provided an escape from the rigours of an imposed style. In 1949 Doisneau was offered and accepted a lucrative contract to work on French *Vogue* magazine, as a fashion photographer. *Vogue's* editor, Michel de Brunhoff, liked Doisneau's work and wished to introduce a new and fresher style of photography into the magazine. Yet the constraints of working in a milieu in which he never felt at ease nagged at Doisneau, and he started to spend his evenings and sometimes whole nights with Giraud, who was fascinated by the lowlife of Paris at night. The contrast between the two activities could not be greater: Doisneau's 'day' job consisted in photographing elegant young women in expensive couture, or in visiting and photographing the sumptuous balls of the rich and famous, while at night he was photographing drunks, *clochards* (tramps), prostitutes, petty criminals and street entertainers in the poorest parts of the city (Pls. 17, 46, 47, 48, 52, 58). The work with Giraud eventually appeared in a couple of books, where Doisneau's photographs are simply employed as illustration, but has never been adequately presented as a coherent project, despite the fame of a number of photographs from this collaboration.[9]

Doisneau did not renew his contract with *Vogue* in 1953 (although he continued to work for the magazine as a freelance from time to time), and the remainder of the 1950s were spent in a wide range of editorial and commercial work. The sheer diversity of his output in this period is summed up by the contact sheet of 1952 (Pl. 18), representing a typical range of commissions: missionaries in the Massif Central, a dormitory in the Salvation army hostel barge on the Seine, an industrial reportage on the SNCASO aircraft factory, and a sumptuous ball for *Vogue*.

The post-war period saw Doisneau's international reputation begin and grow, something helped by his famous Kiss sequence (cover and Pls. 16a and 16b) for *LIFE* magazine in 1950 (of which most are *mises en scènes*). His work was exhibited with that of Willy Ronis, Brassaï and Izis during 1951 at the Museum of Modern Art in New York, and was included by Steichen in the hugely successful *Family of Man* touring exhibition of the mid-1950s.

There is little doubt that the great variety and scope of his work in this period led Doisneau – who was what the French would call a *débrouillard*, someone who sorts things out and gets on with the job – to seek visual short-cuts to achieve effective results. It has been suggested that his friendship with the editor of the magazine *Point de Vue*, Albert Plécy, has something to do with this.[10] As the 1950s progress, it is possible to see Doisneau's compositional style evolve, and certain patterns emerge. For interiors, in particular, he had developed the use of the flashgun, either bounced off the ceiling, or held up above and to the right of the photographer's head to get an oblique 'modelling' light on the subject. Doisneau used a powerful flashbulb (PF56) to get a small stop and thus considerable depth of field – a feeling of 'all-over' clarity – in his pictures (Pl. 43). A frequent approach in his portraits is illustrated by that of the sculptor César Baldaccini (Pl. 44), in which the subject is profiled on the far left foreground, with a characterizing or symbolic element of 'decor' counterposed in the right background. A fascinating version of this technique is furnished by the portrait of Louis Aragon and his wife Elsa Triolet, in which the woman at her desk and the rather haut-bourgeois setting of the room forms the background to Aragon. This photograph is one of a series of portraits in which Doisneau's distaste for the Communist intellectual seems barely disguised. Although Aragon was a surrealist, he was also apparently somewhat haughty, and condescendingly referred on one occasion to Doisneau's career as 'working on populism' ('vous faites dans le populisme').

Doisneau's fascination with literature and stories also provided the means to construct pictures which have a more or less closed narrative structure. In his best work – *La Stricte Intimité, Mlle Anita à la Boule Rouge, Les Enfants de la Place Hébert* – the narrative is quite open and ambiguous. In the photographs which are certainly most popular with a wide public – *Baiser de l'Hôtel de Ville, Le Manège de M. Barré* – the narrative form is very explicit, admitting of a smaller but more immediate range of interpretation. These are also photographs which Doisneau himself finds less rewarding. Pictures of literary or cultural figures often display a similar formulaic quality, using the urban decors of Paris as strong compositional elements to focus attention on a foreground figure. The portraits of André Hardellet (Pl. 78) and Kischka (Pl. 71) exemplify this approach, where the architecture of the city becomes a central element of the photograph. A much 'looser' and more relaxed portrait of Giacometti in a café demonstrates a favoured locale for a Doisneau portrait of this era (Pl. 51). A very interesting example showing how Doisneau made use of the range of his compositional devices is shown in the page of 12 frames of 6 × 6 cm negatives of the writer Raymond Queneau, made on 31 May 1956. The plate (no. 50), a copy of the file cards Doisneau uses to archive his pictures, also shows a number of croppings of the photographs for printing. Although virtually all are impressive portraits of Queneau, the preferred picture was negative no. 42810. By this time Doisneau was frequently turning to the 35 mm camera in order to vary his approach, for, as the Queneau series demonstrates, the fixed lens of the Rolleiflex with which he had worked most often since 1932 was becoming a limiting factor. With a 35 mm camera such as a Leica, other lenses with different angles of view (particularly a wide angle and a 'portrait' telephoto) would make possible a variation of his visual style. Both formats were used by Doisneau (in addition to 5 × 4 in) until the 1970s, but it is instructive to note that a number of important pictures made as early as the first half of the 1950s were in 24 × 36 mm format with a 35 mm wide-angle lens (for example, the young accordeonist in the bistro, 1953, Pl. 52).

Towards the end of the 1950s Doisneau made a fascinating series of photographs for an abortive book project, entitled *Kalou*. This was based on a reportage about transhumance in the Alpes-Maritimes, truly a return

24
An Auvergnat café which also sells coal and fuel-oil, near Porte de Vanves (15^c), Paris, 1971.

25
DATAR project. Deserted playground,
Rosny-sous-Bois, in Seine St-Denis, 1984.

to the landscape of Giono and to the themes which had so entranced the
young Doisneau. He spent some time in the autumn of 1958 accompanying the shepherds and their herds down from the mountains (see photograph of the shepherd Jacques Robion, Pl. 74). But suddenly the reportage
turned into a tragedy. Many years later Jacques Prévert composed a short
text which evokes this period.

TRANSHUMANCE[11]

To Robert

One day in the little mountains of the Alpes-Maritimes, near Entre-
vaux I believe, Robert Doisneau was with a shepherd, his sheep and
his dogs when a wayward lorry decimated the herd, and killed the
two dogs.
'Did you take any photos?'
'No, I consoled the shepherd', replied Doisneau.
And it was as if life, in a snapshot, had made the portrait of
Doisneau.
A simple exchange of worthy processes.
For such a long time already, Robert Doisneau has been making such
beautiful and simply astonishing images, and always on the occasion
of weddings and feasts, of love and the humour of life.

(Autumn 1975)

1960–1978

The number of television sets in French households passed the one million
mark in 1960. As in other Western countries, the inevitable rise of
television during the 1960s dealt a fatal blow to the illustrated press, and
many magazines went into a terminal decline. Advertising revenues fell
and the number of pages devoted to editorial photography was conse-
quently reduced. The demand for humanistic photography fell, for
another generation of young photographers exploiting new styles of reportage was emerging, to compete for the ever-declining pages of the
magazines. Virtually all of the great photographers of Doisneau's generation suffered more or less from these twin assaults on their pre-eminence.
  Doisneau was no exception. He was obliged to turn – as were so many
of his colleagues – to advertising and commercial photography to make his

living. His increasing concentration on a narrative form in his photography enabled him to sell a number of book projects – some designed expressly for children (*Marius le forestier*, 1964, Pl. 84, *Catherine la danseuse*, 1966, Pl. 86, *L'Enfant et la colombe*, 1978) – while others were an attempt to link literary texts with images, such as the little book on scarecrows, *Epouvantables épouvantails*, of 1965 (Pl. 76). But there were also a number of abortive projects, and the critical acclaim for his work that had been abundant in the 1950s was less forthcoming during a period of change to new photographic styles. The post-war generation was coming into its own, exploiting the easy availability of new and cheaper cameras from Japan, with their multiplicity of interchangeable lenses, and better colour films. Doisneau has produced much fine colour work, but his approach is one which perhaps works best in black and white, where the viewer's concentration on the subject is not compromised by another visual register and the involuntary associations which colour generates. A book made with Maurice Chevalier in the early 1970s which contained a good deal of colour proved a disappointment.

The period from the early 1960s to the second half of the 1970s is one of great variety in Doisneau's photography, but it lacks any major or consistent projects to compare with, for example, *La Banlieue de Paris*, and the collaborations with Prévert or Giraud. Yet if anything Doisneau's creativity was accelerating during this time. At the beginning of the 1960s he produced a fascinating collage, *La Maison des locataires*, destined for an exhibition of his photography at the Art Institute of Chicago. This work, Pl. 92, is a simple montage of a number of Doisneau's photographs of Parisians in their own habitat, on a picture of an old apartment building.[12] It is as if the viewer had X-ray vision, able to see into most of the apartments at the same time. *La Maison des locataires* is a sort of microcosm of Doisneau's world, containing a number of characters from what he has called on a number of occasions his *petit théâtre*, and it is possible to see in this work the summation of an important tendency within his photography, that of the attempt to create a sort of literary form through the assembly and association of a certain number of pictures. The books for children such as *Marius, Catherine* and to a lesser extent *L'Enfant et la colombe* are simple and straightforward attempts at a purely narrative photography: *La Maison des locataires* returns to a form glimpsed at in *La Banlieue de Paris*, where the over-all effect of a series of photographs evokes the complex associations of a novel or a poem. A somewhat later and more elaborate work using photographic blocks in relief is shown in Pl. 23 and illustrates the Pont des Arts, the Quais of Paris and the characters to be found in their environs. In this case the effect is more abstract.

Another method for achieving such results is of course furnished by the cinema, and Doisneau would be the first to admit that given different circumstances, he would have liked to become a film director – a *metteur en scène*.

Some at least of the qualities of the film director are also evident in the advertising work which Doisneau produced. He employed some interesting techniques to produce visually exciting results – notably the turntable and the modified focal plane shutter of a 5×4 inch camera to make the 'twisting' pictures of couples (Pl. 22). A collaboration with another photographer, Jacques Dubois, led to a series of advertising pictures using coloured gels projected on a studio backdrop, and a number of other interesting visual effects which helped to ensure that Doisneau received a steady flow of advertising commissions. In the early 1970s he invented a type of periphery camera to make pictures of circular objects for an interesting private book commission on *Métiers de tradition* (traditional crafts). Throughout the period Doisneau continued to make solitary promenades through Paris and the *banlieue*, and to make pictures for his own interest (Pls. 81, 82 and 85).

The quasi-revolution of May 1968 in Paris passed Doisneau by, for he was laid out at the time with a classic injury for photographers – a slipped disc. This was frustrating for him, less because he would have been attracted to photographing the events, than because this historic event symbolized the triumph of *désobéissance* over the established order. Few of the humanistic photographers made pictures of the May events (although Cartier-Bresson was an exception), and its recording was largely left to the younger generation, notably photographers like Gilles Caron and Bruno Barbey.

The post-1968 world did, however, produce a mounting interest in photography in France, and it began to revive interest in reportage photography of the type practised by Doisneau. In 1977 he was commissioned to make another book, this time on the Loire.

It was not an easy commission, although it certainly offered the possibility of making the more 'literary' type of study which Doisneau found most congenial. His wife had fallen ill, and he could not absent himself from Paris for the periods of concentrated work which such a commission really demanded. None the less the project produced some interesting photographs (Pls. 80, 88–91). Although Doisneau counts it as a relative failure, it was to prove that the audience and appeal of his photography was widening again.

42

1978–1992

Two factors have contributed to a renaissance in Doisneau's photography in the period since the late 1970s. Firstly, Doisneau has been rediscovered by a larger and more visually sophisticated audience than was available for his photography in the 1960s or 1970s. Secondly, his increasing public prominence in France produced a surfeit of interesting commissions, almost a return to the situation of the 1940s and 1950s, for it brought in its wake encounters with several important figures from the worlds of literature, film and the performing arts.

During the early 1980s the post-war generation, now in control of the cultural institutions of French society, rediscovered with a certain nostalgia the major figures of humanistic photography. The publication of a retrospective volume, *Trois secondes d'éternité*, in 1979 was followed in 1983 by the *Photopoche* volume on Doisneau's work (the best-selling title in the series). The first confirmed Doisneau's importance to the photographic establishment, the second introduced him to a large and predominantly youthful audience. A welter of exhibitions, books and articles have followed, and Doisneau became a media figure in his own right – not least because he was an entertaining and amusing speaker, a character who was eminently 'mediatisable'.

Although not new to photography for the cinema, the opportunity to do a reportage on the filming of Bertrand Tavernier's *Un Dimanche à la campagne* in 1983 introduced Doisneau to the actress Sabine Azema, who has become both a sort of muse and the subject of a number of great photographs (Pls. 99 and 105). In 1992 Azema and Doisneau made a jointly directed film about Doisneau's life.

The new-found respectability of photography, and a generous level of public funding from the Mitterand government, led to the setting up in 1983–4 of a large-scale group project on the French landscape for a state body, the DATAR.[13] During 1984–5 Doisneau contributed a study of the *banlieue* and new towns (*villes nouvelles*) of the Paris region to the DATAR. Some of his photography on this project took him back to the areas traversed in the 1930s and 1940s for *La Banlieue de Paris*, but he also went further afield, exploring the east and west of Paris. This time, however, he made many of the pictures in colour and focused on the built environment. Doisneau was especially interested in showing the consequences of what he called the 'arrogance' of modern architecture for those who lived in the *banlieue* and *villes nouvelles* of the 1980s, and felt it could be his last chance to carry out a major photographic study.

26
The ex-Au Bon Coin (see Pl. 15), St-Denis, in 1987.

27
In front of the HBM buildings constructed in
the 1920s, Gentilly, 1989.

The resulting pictures depict an environment almost entirely transformed in the period since the 1940s. A process of *embourgeoisement* has taken place, and it is this, coupled with the near universality of the car, which has privatized the area to such an extent that, at least in these photographs, the individual rarely appears on the streets or in the public spaces. Doisneau's view is of a bleak and dehumanized urban environment (Pls. 25, 95). Where in the 1930s children played on the *terrains vagues*, now they are hardly to be seen, even in the spaces specially built for their use. And in a moment of supreme irony, one of Doisneau's own pictures of the 1950s – Braque at Varengeville (Pl. 41) – looks down on the photographer from where it has been painted on to the side of an anonymous concrete block (Pl. 93).

The *banlieue* was not Doisneau's first choice of subject for the DATAR, but at the time his wife had become seriously ill and he did not want to leave Montrouge to carry out his preferred project, on industrial decline in Eastern France. Photographing the new towns and their massive architectural follies, however, was possible through an extended series of day trips. Doisneau's approach was highly 'considered' for he used a medium format 6 × 7 cm camera, mounted on a tripod, producing images whose clarity and great compositional power seem infused with an overwhelming sense of pessimism. Yet the opportunity to collaborate in a team project with a number of younger photographers proved a turning point, revitalizing his whole approach.

The 'return to the *banlieue*' in Doisneau's work continued until the end of his life, but progressively revealed a more humanized environment, as if to revise the judgement of the DATAR pictures. In the two final long-term projects, one on St-Denis, the other on Gentilly, we find Doisneau portraying again the children, couples, workers, street entertainers, and popular festivals which animated his earlier vision of the *banlieue* (Pls. 26, 27, 94, 96–8, 100–4, 106, 107). In his last pictures it is as if the story of the *classe populaire* had been resumed, as if our 'author' had found again in its modern expression the vitality which had enchanted him when he first explored the *zone*, back in his childhood.

Robert Doisneau continued to lead a busy life as a photographer until October 1993, when he fell ill. He died in April 1994, his work still widely in demand, his photography marked by a fascination with those with whom he had the most profound of affinities, the ordinary people of Paris and its suburbs. His pictures of them were a form of self-portrait.

¹ This aphorism, which Robert Doisneau used for the title of his autobiography, translates as 'You conjugate the verb ''to photograph'' with the imperfect of the objective.' The allusion to the apparent objectivity of photography and the subjective imperfections to which it is prey is coupled with a reference to the imprecisions of the camera itself (*objectif* also means lens in French). It is unfortunately impossible to translate the aphorism into English and retain its full meaning.

² Cited in Jean-François Chevrier, *Robert Doisneau*, Editions Belfond, Paris, 1983, p. 33.

³ Gamma is a term used in photographic sensitometry to denote the contrast index of a negative.

⁴ Vigneau and Doisneau made the photograph for the cover of Simenon's first Maigret novel.

⁵ In Robert Doisneau, *Doisneau-Renault*, Editions Hazan, Paris, 1988.

⁶ Many of the photographs taken for this project were reprinted in Robert Doisneau, *La Science de Doisneau*, Editions Hoëbeke, Paris, 1989.

⁷ Much of the treatment of humanistic photography contained in this section owes a considerable debt to the research of Mme Marie de Thèzy, of the Bibliothèque Historique de la Ville de Paris.

⁸ 'Le livre sur la banlieue [...] c'est mon portrait. Comme lui je suis un agglomérat de scories.' Quoted in Jean-François Chevrier, *Robert Doisneau*, pp. 37–8.

⁹ Robert Giraud's book about his life among the *bas-fonds*, *Le Vin des rues*, which Prévert was instrumental in getting published in 1955, was reissued by Denoël in 1983 with a number of Doisneau's pictures of the period.

¹⁰ Chevrier makes this case quite convincingly in relation to the book of Doisneau's pictures that Plécy edited, *Instantanés de Paris* (1955).

¹¹ Jacques Prévert, *La Pluie et le beau temps*, Gallimard, Paris, 1981, p. 219.

¹² A fascinating discussion of *La Maison des locataires* can be found in Sylvain Roumette, *Lettre à un aveugle sur les photographies de Robert Doisneau*, Le Tout sur Le Tout/Le Temps qu'il Fait, Paris/Cognac, 1990.

¹³ Délégation à l'Aménagement du Territoire et à l'Action Régionale. The project was an initiative of the photographer François Hers and the planner Bernard Latarget. The group project was published as *Paysages photographiés en France des années quatre-vingt*, Paris, Editions Hazan/DATAR, 1989.

28
One of Doisneau's first photographs, Gentilly,
1929 or 1930.

29
Anglers on quai de Seine, near Pont Mirabeau,
Paris 15ᵉ, 1932.

30
Football in the street, Ave. Auguste-Comte,
Paris 6ᵉ, 1937

31
Lavoir municipal (Village Wash-tank),
Dordogne, 1937.

32
Advertising photograph for Renault, 1936.

33
Canoe holiday, abortive reportage for Charles
Rado's agency Rapho (Doisneau's wife
Pierrette is in canoe at right), Dordogne,
1939.

34
Deux femmes sur un diable, St-Eustache (Two Women on a Market-porter's Handcart, near St-Eustache Church, Les Halles Market), Paris 4ᵉ, 1932.

35
Les Petits Enfants au lait (*Two Children fetching the Milk*), Gentilly, 1932.

36
La Descente à l'usine (*Down to the Factory*), 1946.

37
Meilleur Ouvrier de France (Best Craftsman of France), 1942.

38
Manufacture of Clarinets, Paris, 1943.

LE 19 AOUT 1944, PARIS SE
SOULEVE CONTRE LES OCCU-
PANTS NAZIS A DEUX HEURES
DE L'APRES-MIDI, LA BA-
TAILLE EST ENGAGEE AUX
QUATRE COINS DE LA VILLE...

**21 AOUT 1944
LIBÉRATION
DE PARIS**

NOTRE PHOTOGRAPHE

...QUAI SAINT-MICHEL, LE PRE-
MIER CAMION ALLEMAND EST
ATTAQUE ET REDUIT EN
CENDRES. AUJOURD'HUI AU
MEME LIEU UN GROUPE D'EN-
FANTS INSOUCIANTS PASSE.

2

39
'Notre Photographe a fait le Même
Reportage . . .' ('Our photographer
has carried out the same reportage'),
a magazine spread from *Point de Vue*
comparing Doisneau's photographs
made during the liberation of Paris
with those made from the same
locations three years later, 1947.

58

BOULEVARD SAINT-MICHEL ON DRESSE LES PREMIERES BARRICADES. AUJOURD'HUI LE BOULEVARD VIT AU RYTHME DE PAIX.

SAINT MICHEL, LE PECHEUR A LA LIGNE A REMPLACE   LE F. F. I. QUI PORTE SON FUSIL COMME UNE CANNE A PECHE.

AIT LE MÊME REPORTAGE...

AUX TUILERIES, UN CHAR TIGRE EST TOUCHE A MORT. 4 ANS APRES, LES ENFANTS DANSENT LA RONDE A LA MEME PLACE.

SUITE AU VERSO

59

40
A clandestine press of the Parisian Resistance.
Doisneau's friend the painter Enrico
Pontremoli at centre, his wife at right,
another painter (Philbert) at left. Reportage
for *Le Point*, 1945.

41
Georges Braque à Varengeville, reportage for *Le Point*, Normandy, 1953.

42
La Tireuse de cartes (*The Fortune Teller*), Paris
4ᵉ, 1951.

43
M. Nollan chez lui (*Monsieur Nollan at Home,
surrounded by his possessions, mostly copies or
things picked up in the flea market*), Paris 6ᵉ,
1950.

47
Richardo, the tattooed man, picture made in Doisneau's apartment (his children hid under the bed when they caught sight of Richardo), Montrouge, 1949.

46
Tattooed man, Prison-Hospice de Nanterre, Nanterre, 1952.

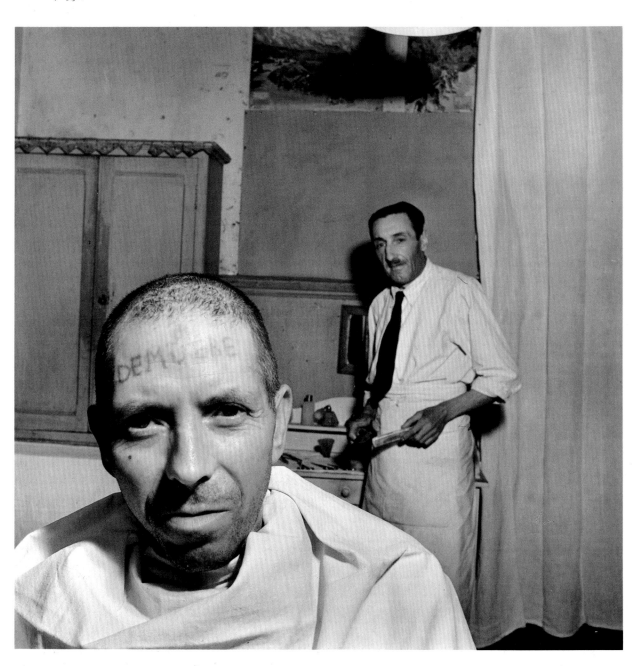

48
Coco, Paris, 1952.

49
Mademoiselle Anita à la Boule Rouge, Paris 11ᵉ,
1951.

50
Contact sheets of a portrait session with the
writer Raymond Queneau, 31 May 1956, near
rue Reuilly, Paris, 12ᵉ, 1956.

51
Alberto Giacometti, in a café near his studio,
rue d'Alésia, Paris 14ᵉ, 1958.

53

L'Accordéoniste, rue Mouffetard, Paris 5ᵉ, 1951.

52

The young accordeonist and her companion,
café in Les Halles area, Paris 2ᵉ, 1953.

54

Maurice Baquet et l'homme orchestre (Maurice Baquet and the one-man-band, M. Vermondel), Paris 18ᵉ, 1957.

Course à la valise (Suitcase Race), Athis-Mons,
Essonne, 1945.

56
Boule Championships of France, Roanne,
1950.

57
La Trépidante Wanda (*The Gyrating Wanda*),
Paris 14e, 1953.

59
Mademoiselle Vivin, nude dancer at the
Concert Mayol, goes shopping, Faubourg
St-Martin, Paris 10ᵉ, 1953.

58
Monsieur Georges et Riton, rue Watt, Paris 13ᵉ,
1953.

60
Bistro at Arcueil, 1945.

61
Wedding at Gerbeviller (reportage for *Vogue*),
France, 1949.

62
Le Ruban de la mariée (*The Wedding Ribbon*),
traditional marriage ritual in Poitou, Vienne,
1951.

63
La Stricte Intimité (*In the Strictest Intimacy*), rue
Marcelin Berthelot, Montrouge, 1945.

65

Le Manège de Monsieur Barré (M. Barré's Roundabout), Paris, 1955.

64

Monsieur Flinois, Bouquiniste (second-hand bookdealer) in front of Notre-Dame, Paris 5ᵉ, 1951.

67

Les Gosses de la Place Hébert (Kids at the Place Hébert), Paris 18ᵉ, 1957.

66

Enfant sage dans cour de récréation (Cissy in the Playground), Paris, 1954.

68
Jacques Prévert, Ave. D'Orléans (now Ave.
Gen. Leclerc), Paris 18ᵉ, 1955.

69
Georges Simenon outside a concierge's office,
Paris, 1962.

70
The inventor Paul Arzens with his car, Paris,
1951.

71
The painter Kischka, Canal St-Denis, 1958.

Usine de gaz à Cornillon (Gas Works at Cornillon), St-Denis, 1955.

73
Les Deux Couronnes (*The Two Wreaths*),
Marseilles, 1955.

74
Jacques Robion, shepherd in the Alpes-
Maritimes, 1958.

75
*Les Spécialistes de la Maison Gougeon installent les
statues de Maillol aux Tuileries (Specialists from
the firm of Gougeon installing Maillol statues in
the Tuileries Gardens), Paris, 1964*

76
Epouvantail (*Scarecrow*), Dordogne, 1965.

96

The writer André Hardellet, under Autoroute
A6 at Gentilly, 1975.

79
Multiple-exposure picture for *La Vie Ouvrière*,
illustrating article on industrial injuries,
1977.

81
Francine Doisneau in a café at Ave. Jean-Jaurès, Paris 17ᵉ, 1971.

80
Young motorcyclists at Château de Chambord,
Loir-et-Cher, 1977.

82
Near Notre-Dame, Paris 5^c, 1969.

84
Marius le forestier (Marius the Forest-guard),
Normandy, 1963.

86
Catherine la danseuse (*Catherine the Dancer*),
Paris, 1965.

87
Maurice Baquet, Montrouge, 1964.

88
Policemen and Firemen, Langeais, Indre-et-
Loire, 1977.

89
Pont de Nevers, Nièvre, 1977.

90
Pepère et Memère (*Grandpa and Grandma*), M.
and Mme Château-Body at Parnay, Indre-et-
Loire, 1977.

91

Les Rochers de L'Espinasse, which resemble an enormous chameleon under their carpet of snow, Haute-Loire, 1977.

92
La Maison des locataires, 1962.

93
DATAR project. Braque at Varengeville (see
Pl. 41), painted on the wall of building at
Argenteuil, 1984.

94
Cité du Franc-Moisin, St-Denis, 1987.

95
DATAR project. Noisy-le Grand, 1984.

96
Canal St-Denis, St-Denis, 1987.

98
Fête du Lendit, le petit Marcel (Fair of the Lendit, little Marcel), St-Denis, 1986.

99
On the set of *Un Dimanche à la campagne*,
Sabine Azema in foreground, 1983.

100
Market at the Place Jean-Jaurès, St-Denis,
1986.

101
Gentilly, 1990.

102

Madame Nenette et Monsieur Antoine, Chez Antoine, Gentilly, 1990.

123

103

Les Deux Garagistes (The Two Garage Mechanics), Gentilly, 1990.

104
The collector of *manèges* (roundabouts),
Gentilly, 1991.

105
Sabine Azema at Chez Gegène, Joinville,
1985.

106
Gentilly, 1990.

BIBLIOGRAPHY

This list is confined to the main publications of Robert Doisneau's photographs and writings. A more extensive if somewhat dated bibliography will be found in the Robert Doisneau entry in *Contemporary Photographers*, St James's Press, New York, 1989.

1949 *La Banlieue de Paris,* text by Blaise Cendrars, Editions Pierre Seghers, Paris.

1952 *Sortilège de Paris* (13 photos by Doisneau), text by François Cali, Arthaud, Paris.

1954 *Les Parisiens tels qu'ils sont*, text by Robert Giraud and Michel Ragon, Delpire, Paris.

1955 *Instantanés de Paris*, preface by Albert Plécy, Editions Claire-Fontaine, Lausanne.

1956 *Gosses de Paris*, text by Jean Dongues, Editions Jeheber, Paris.

1956 *Pour que Paris soit*, text by Elsa Triolet, Editions du Cercle d'Art, Paris.

1962 *Nicolas Schöffer* (30 photos by Doisneau), introduction by Jean Cassou, text by Guy Habasque and Dr Jacques Ménétrier, Editions du Griffon, Neuchâtel.

1964 *Marius le forestier*, text by Dominique Halevy, Fernand Nathan, Paris.

1965 *Le Royaume d'Argot* (40 photos by Doisneau), text by Robert Giraud, editions Denoël, Paris.

1965 *Epouvantables épouvantails* (25 photos by Doisneau), texts chosen by Jean-François Chabrun, Editions Hors Mesure, Paris.

1966 *Catherine la danseuse*, text by Michèle Manceaux, Fernand Nathan, Paris.

1966 *Métiers de Tradition* (60 photos by Doisneau), preface by Georges-Henri Rivière, Edition hors-commerce (Crédit Lyonnais).

1966 Reduced edition (24 photos) of *La Banlieue de Paris,* text by Blaise Cendrars, Editions Pierre Seghers, Paris.

1971 *Témoins de la vie quotidienne* (286 photos by Doisneau), Edition hors-commerce (Crédit Lyonnais).

1972 *Mon Paris*, text by Maurice Chevalier, MacMillan Co, New York.

1974 *Le Paris de Robert Doisneau et Max-Pol Fouchet*, Les Editeurs Français Réunis, Paris.

1978 *L'Enfant et la colombe*, text by James Sage, Editions du Chêne, Paris.

1978 *La Loire* (42 photos), Editions Denoël, Paris.

1979 *Trois secondes d'éternité*, Contrejour, Paris.

1979 *Le Mal de Paris*, text by Clement Lepidis, Arthaud, Paris.

1981 *Ballade pour violoncelle et chambre noire* with Maurice Baquet, Editions Herscher, Paris.

1981 *Passages et galeries du 19ᵉ siècle*, text by Bernard Delvaille, Balland, Paris.

1982 *Robert Doisneau*, J.-F. Chevrier, Belfond, Paris.

1983 3rd edition, by Editions Denoël, Paris, of *La Banlieue de Paris.*

1983 *Le Vin des rues*, Robert Giraud (56 photos by Doisneau), Editions Denoël, Paris.

1983 *Robert Doisneau*, text by Sylvian Roumette, Collection Photopoche, Centre Nationale de Photographie, Paris. (English language edition 1991 published by Thames and Hudson, London.)

1986 *Un Certain Robert Doisneau*, Editions du Chêne, Paris.

1988 *Doisneau-Renault*, Editions Hazan, Paris. (English edition published by Dirk Nishen, London, 1990.)

Bonjour Monsieur le Corbusier, text Jean Petit, Editions Hans Grieshafer, Zurich.

1989 *La Science de Doisneau*, Editions Hoëbeke, Paris.

1989 *Paysages photographiés en France des années quatre-vingt* (21 photos by Doisneau), Editions Hazan/DATAR, Paris.

1989 *Les Doigts pleins d'encre*, Editions Hoëbeke, Paris.

1989 *A l'imparfait de l'objectif: souvenirs et portraits*, Editions Pierre Belfond, Paris.

1990 2nd edn. of 1979. *Trois secondes d'éternité*, Contrejour, Paris.

1990 *Les Auvergnats*, Jacques Dubois (includes 40 photos by Doisneau), Nathan, Paris.

1990 *Lettre à un aveugle sur des photographies de Robert Doisneau*, Sylvian Roumette (41 photos by Doisneau), Le Tout sur le Tout/Le Temps qu'il fait, Paris/Cognac.

1991 *Les Grandes Vacances*, Editions Hoëbeke, Paris.

1991 *La Compagnie des zincs*, Seghers, Paris.

1991 *Portrait de St-Denis*, Calmann-Levy Paris.

1992 *Mes gens de plume*, textes sélectionnés par Yvonne Dubois, Editions de La Martinière, Paris.

1992 *Rue Jacques Prévert*, Editions Hoëbeke, Paris.

1993 *La vie de famille*, texte de Daniel Pennac, Editions Hoëbeke, Paris.

1994 *Doisneau 40/44*, texte de Pascal Ory, Editions Hoëbeke, Paris.

1995 *Robert Doisneau: La vie d'un photographe*, texte de Peter Hamilton, Editions Hoëbeke, Paris.

1995 *Robert Doisneau: A Photographer's Life*, text by Peter Hamilton, Abbeville Press, New York.